Teenagers in a Monastery... ...Yeah RIGHT!

Andrew Nicholson
with contributions from members of the
Cornwall Methodist /Anglican Youth Synod

CPH
Cowethas
Publishing House

First Published 2007 by Cowethas Publishing House,
Tresillian, Truro, Cornwall TR2 4BE

Cover design Jeremy Waters & Andrew Nicholson
Front cover photograph of Pentecost Stained Glass Window at Taizé.
Photography by Andrew Nicholson
Printing by Mid Cornwall Printing, Truro from supplied originals.

A catalogue record for this book is available from the British Library

ISBN 978-0-9556427-08

Forward by Brother James of the Taizé Community

> Then many nations shall come and say: "Come, let us go up to the mountain of the Lord, to the house of the God of Jacob; that he may teach us his ways and that we may walk in his paths." *Micah 4:2*

Taizé is, in fact, not on a mountain - but it *is* on a small hill. It's also not the only place where you might go to meet God, but every week of the year people from many nations come here, just like the young people whose thoughts and feelings fill these pages.

Why do they come? Well, perhaps it's not for me to answer that question. Brother Roger, the founder of our community felt very strongly that young people should be left the space to speak in their own words.

He liked to express his own thoughts in short prayers which he wrote for the common prayer times each day in Taizé and maybe that's the most appropriate way to introduce this book, in prayer, with a prayer which expresses the heart of what we would like to live together:

"Bless us, Lord Christ;
us and those you have entrusted to us.
Keep us in the spirit of the Beatitudes,
joyful,
simple,
full of mercy."
from "The Sources of Taizé"

Acknowledgements

Thank you to Jeremy and all the team at Mid Cornwall Printing for your professionalism, friendliness, and above all, patience. Thanks to the Taizé Community for the unceasing welcome you offer to the many thousands who visit from across the world each year. Thanks especially to Brother James at Taizé for taking the time to contribute to this book. Thanks to the young people featured in these pages, which I had the privilege of taking to Taizé; and to Jacquie, Steve, Lorraine, and my wife, Helen, for your invaluable help in making the trip possible. Also thank you Helen for your repeated prods and reminders (!), which have helped to galvanise me into making the idea of this book into reality. Finally, thanks to God for all He has done in my life, and for giving me Isaac – my wonderful baby boy.

Dedication

This book is dedicated to the memory of Bernadette Breslin who showed such passion in encouraging young people from Britain to discover the miracle of Taizé. Thank you Bernie, you made so many life changing experiences possible.

What's this all about? – Preface

After our pilgrimage to Taizé, Easter 2006, when I had finally said goodbye to the last of the teenage pilgrims, I sat in a hotel room in Exeter and read what the young people wrote about the week they had had, I was so moved by the power of their experiences that I knew they couldn't be left to gather dust on a shelf; these were a remarkable collection of stories that demanded to be heard. This book of testimonies has been compiled so that you too may be inspired to visit this amazing place (or to take your own youth or young adult group). It might just change your life.

Andrew Nicholson

On our way – The Cornwall Youth Synod by the River Seine in Paris.

Taizé Community – A Brief History

The Taizé Community was founded by Brother Roger, who moved to the tiny village of Taizé, France from his home in Switzerland in 1940. Aged just twenty five, he felt that God was calling him to live out a life of peace and reconciliation within a community. Taizé was chosen due to its proximity to the demarcation boarder which cut France in two during the Second World War, and he believed that this community could be a presence of hope within the sufferings of the time. At great personal risk, he began hiding refugees – mostly Jewish from the Nazis - and he narrowly evaded capture himself. After the war he was joined in this search by others, and in 1949 the first Brothers of Taizé made a commitment to live a common life of celibacy, community of possessions, and simplicity in life.

Today there are over one hundred Brothers, uniquely consisting of monks from both protestant AND catholic backgrounds, from more than twenty five different countries. The Community is a living parable of hope and reconciliation between divided nations and a divided church. Some of the Brothers live overseas alongside some of the world's poorest communities, striving to be a presence of hope and love.

From the late 1950s onwards, visitors began to stay with the Taizé Community in ever increasing numbers. The Community were soon unable to accommodate everyone in the local village church for communal prayer, so a massive new church – the Church of Reconciliation - was built on the hill above the village. This too has had to be extended several times over the years; such has been the influx of visitors. Today tens of thousands make a pilgrimage to stay in Taizé each year, with as many as 5-6000 staying in the peak Easter and summer weeks, from up to 80 different countries at any one time. Amazingly, the vast majority of these pilgrims are teenagers and young adults, searching for meaning in their lives in communion with others. Interestingly, the Brothers do not see themselves as some kind of spiritual masters, instead they invite young people in particular, to join with them in their search to live out God's call at the very heart of each human being.

So exactly what is this fascination that draws such vast numbers to this remote French village? Why is it so compelling? A young American girl featured on the "Week at Taizé"[1] video gives a possible clue: "I've heard countless sermons about prayer – you can do this, you can do that - but at Taizé they just let you do it!".

[1] A week at Taizé© A & PT, 71250 Taizé Communauté, France 1999.

Within the routine of monastic life, young people are frequently amazed to discover an inner freedom. A freedom to explore who they truly are, a freedom to share that builds trust with those from different nations, a freedom from all the distractions of an increasingly material world, a freedom to encounter the mystery of God's presence personally.

This book is a series of testimonies from one such pilgrimage. Where (for once!), young people are encouraged to take responsibility by "just doing it"!

Groups from around the world meeting together.

Andrew's Dairy, My Hopes and Expectations:-

Monday

It's 15.22 and we're hurtling towards Macon from Paris on the TGV. The Youth Synod trip from Cornwall to Taizé is really happening! Despite the confusion with our flight confirmation which threatened to undermine the whole trip, we've been brought through that, and we're now coming back the following Monday, twenty four hours later.

The Taizé evening we had at Youth Synod was brilliant. There was such a profound sense of God's presence there that evening, and I really felt a sense of conviction about the vision for this trip. It's amazing to look up and actually have twenty of us all going – the interest was backed up by action.

I wonder what God has in store for each of them over the course of the next week? I remember how deeply I was moved and affected by Taizé on my first visit in 1998, and all of the times since. It is such a powerful experience of God's love being lived out in community.

There is going to be a sense of sadness too. Eleven months ago I visited Taizé and Brother Roger was the leader of the Community, just as he had been since its inception. Only months later, the unthinkable happened – he was murdered during evening prayer. It still sounds ridiculous to write this, even now. His memory and the legacy of his life will live on; yet it feels like there will be something missing. He started all this from a humble "Yes" to God in service. I'm not sure how I will feel to sit there and see where he used to sit, empty. His death really shook me very deeply, and yet God's work continues. Now there is a Community of more than a hundred who have responded with their own "Yes", and through their service they have enabled tens of thousands of people to discover their own calling - their own way of responding, their own "Yes".

Brother Roger's grave.

My prayer for this week is that this group

of young people will discover something of the call that God has put in the heart of each of us for themselves. That through all that goes on in Taizé, they will be touched by God's presence, that they will meet with Him. And where will that encounter lead? Hopefully to a "Yes" of their very own; at the very heart of who they truly are.

I wonder what they are all hoping for?!

A Day In The Life Of Taizé:-
In order to make sense of the testimonies in this book, it is important to set the context as to what actually takes place in a typical week (if there can be such a thing!) in Taizé. Sundays are the change over days where thousands of pilgrims either arrive or depart (although for the week after Easter and at Pentecost it is Monday). Not surprisingly, it's pretty chaotic as groups all descend from across the globe at once, but each group is welcomed in their own language, and answers are provided to questions about accommodation, food and the programme. The following day, things settle down and a familiar rhythm to the day develops as the week progresses.

07.45 – Bells ring
08.20 – Morning Prayer
09.00 – Breakfast
10.00 – Bible introduction
11.00 – Free time/personal reflection
12.30 – Midday Prayer
13.00 – Lunch
14.00 – Optional song practice/free time
15.30 – Discussion Groups
17.15 – Snack
17.45 – Workshops
19.00 – Supper
20.30 – Evening Prayer
21.30 – Oyak

Within this structure there is also a time when groups meet others from their own country, and groups also have the opportunity to arrange a meeting with one of the Brothers where they can ask questions and find out more about how it is possible to live in a Community like this. In the summer months a world forum takes place on Saturday afternoon which provides a fascinating mixture of cultural entertainment from around the globe.

Cornwall Youth Synod group with Brother Paolo.

The key elements which make up a week in Taizé:

The Prayer

Three times a day in Taizé, everyone stops what they are doing and they come together to pray in the church. How is this possible when there are so many different traditions and languages? The prayer takes on a very distinctive and accessible form of chanting, silence, and intercession. Teaching takes place elsewhere. The songs of Taizé are known across different denominations throughout the world. They are actually chants - short, simple phrases proclaiming biblical truths - which are sung in different languages. Each is sung and repeated a number of times, and many people find that something remarkable happens: they experience a profound sense of God's peace through some kind of mysterious awakening of the soul. The relatively long period of silence in the middle of the prayer (up to ten minutes) is quite alien to most Christian traditions of communal worship. Yet this time of waiting and listening, is at the very heart of the spiritual life in Taizé. Everyone stops, everyone waits on God together. Many young people are astounded to discover that by the end of their stay, this silence is one of the most special parts of the whole week. They are free to discover and encounter God's presence for themselves – there's no-one to get in the way.

The Teaching

There are various themes you can choose to follow through your week in Taizé. Each group has a daily reflection with one of the Brothers who introduce a piece of scripture which leads to some thought provoking questions. Groups of around a dozen are formed, mixing nationalities, and the questions are discussed together. Remarkably, young people from different parts of the world are able to share some of their most intimate thoughts on the meaning of their lives, in spite (or because?) of language and cultural differences. Groups are assembled so that everyone can hopefully understand in one common language, with someone within a group able to translate where necessary. Initial barriers quickly melt away and young people find great benefit in being able to explore the Christian faith together.

The Sharing – Living And Sharing In Community Together

The task of providing for a ever changing community of up to several thousand at time is an immense challenge. Many of the Brothers and permanent helpers are involved full time with the many tasks that are needed to help to make communal life work. But life together is only possible with the willingness of visitors to lend a hand in the day to day running. So each small group is given a task for the week. These tasks could include food distribution, washing up, litter clearing, cleaning, jobs in the church and helping with the welcome of new visitors. Somehow, tasks that would seem most unappealing at home can become great sources of team bonding and fun when tackled together (even cleaning the toilet!!). It really is a living parable of community, for everyone depends on each other for life to be possible together. In Taizé, the feeding of the five thousand is just one of many little miracles that occur each day!

Brother James leading a discussion.

Workshops

During the week in Taizé, there are a range of workshops on offer featuring different themes and topics. These could be as diverse as a speaker on economic development or international affairs, a biblical theme, icons, art, drawing, music, or presentations of different cultures and countries, which invariably include much colour, song, dancing, not to mention participation!

Oyak

Surely Taizé is the only monastery in the world with its own café/bar! Oyak is the unofficial DIY entertainment and social centre of Taizé. Only open during certain times of the day, it truly comes to life in the evening after Evening Prayer. It is a remarkable exchange of cultures, friendship, music, games and dance, particularly so in the busy Easter or peak summer weeks. Often groups of several hundred at a time will enthusiastically gather around a large posse of guitarists, singing for their lives. Personally, I will never forget the experience of dancing in a conga line behind an Italian man playing the bag pipes!

A typical scene of fun at Oyak.

QUESTIONS TO PONDER:-

Towards the end of the week, the young people from the Cornwall Youth Synod were given the opportunity to reflect on their time in Taizé.They were given four questions to prompt feedback:

- **How has Taizé affected you?**

- **What has happened to you this week that you want to remember?**

- **Has God spoken to you this week, and if so how?**

- **Have you discovered anything new about yourself, God, or community?**

Entirely in their own creatively chosen words (!), this is what **Teenagers in a Monastery** had to say:

How can I describe Taize?
Amazing, fantastic, unforgetable.

I wasn't sure about it before I came and last week there were points that I wish I wasn't coming. its never been my thing - beig quiet, and I didn't think that the worship was for me, all my life i've prefered to worship in a loud, fun and exciting way, and I didn't think that that was what Taize was at all, I thought i was not going to enjoy it atall. But by Thursday / friday →

I started to understand it, I started to realise that it was possible to connect with God through Silence + chanting → I've learnt that this can be fun and exciting too, it is possible to be loud in other ways at Taize, and to reach god through their style of worship! It was on the friday nights worship with the cross that I finally understood it, I felt that it was possibly the first time →

over that I have managed to use prayer to effectively talk to god, because it allways has seemed to me that you need to tell god what you want him to know, but now I know that you can use prayer to just talk to him and find solutions to my problems rather than just tell them to him!

But alongside the prayer sessions I am never going to forget the experiance of Taize, my group was →

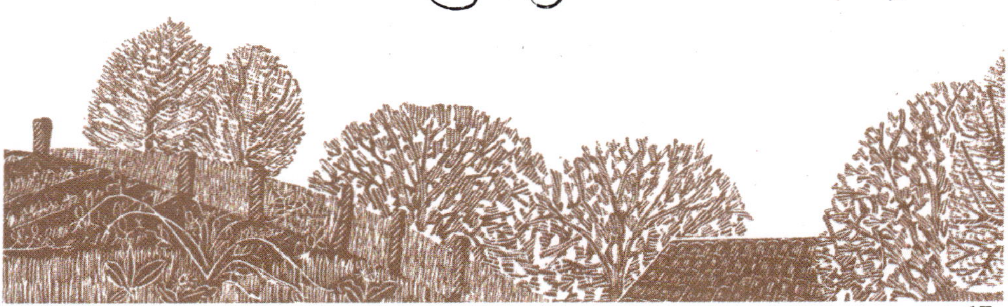

me and 10 Germans +
a German Leader at
first it was weird but
by the end of the week
i feel that i have gotten
to know and understand
another culture + I like
it! I've made so, so many
new friends this week -
English, German, French
and Australian. I didn't
even mind the food! It
was a Great experiance
that I'm never going to
forget => Thanks Taize!

Ohhh Hamish the
Hamster

Sorry for
rambeling => i couldn't stop
talking about it - it wa
so great!

This week
at taize has changed my view on worship. before i came here i thought that the only way that i could contact god was to sing loud and have a party but now i see that Peace can make a deeper connection. Taize has effected me in a way that has helped me to understand my self. it has helped me to identify my weaknesses as a person and has shown me a way to change them into strengths. The thing i want to remember this week is how simple life can be if you just slow down and that a simple life doesn't mean unhappyness →

I dont feel that god has spoken directly to me but has shown me his concerns through the people i have met as they all have qualities that i should strive to acquire. sorry for rambeling i was bored and had nothing else to do

Love

Lucie ....

the limpit.

-x-

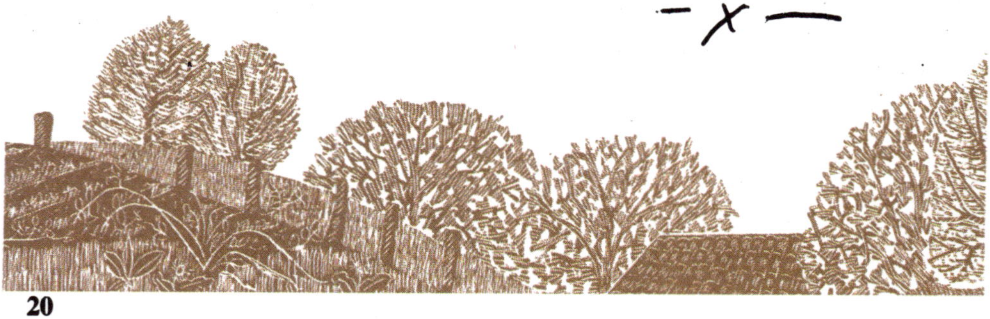

At the
beginning
of the week ~~e~~ I was expecting it
to be really dull and I wouldn't be
able to stay ~~quite~~ quiet. but now
I Love it and am looking forward
to coming back soon for longer. I
really enjoyed being able to go~~ing~~back
after dyak and just lying down and
praying. I really enjoyed meeting
new people but it was sad to
say goodbye. Im really glad I came
because i really needed a spirital
up lift which Im glad to say I
got. It was an amazing time and
loved every mintue of it

Mel
-x-

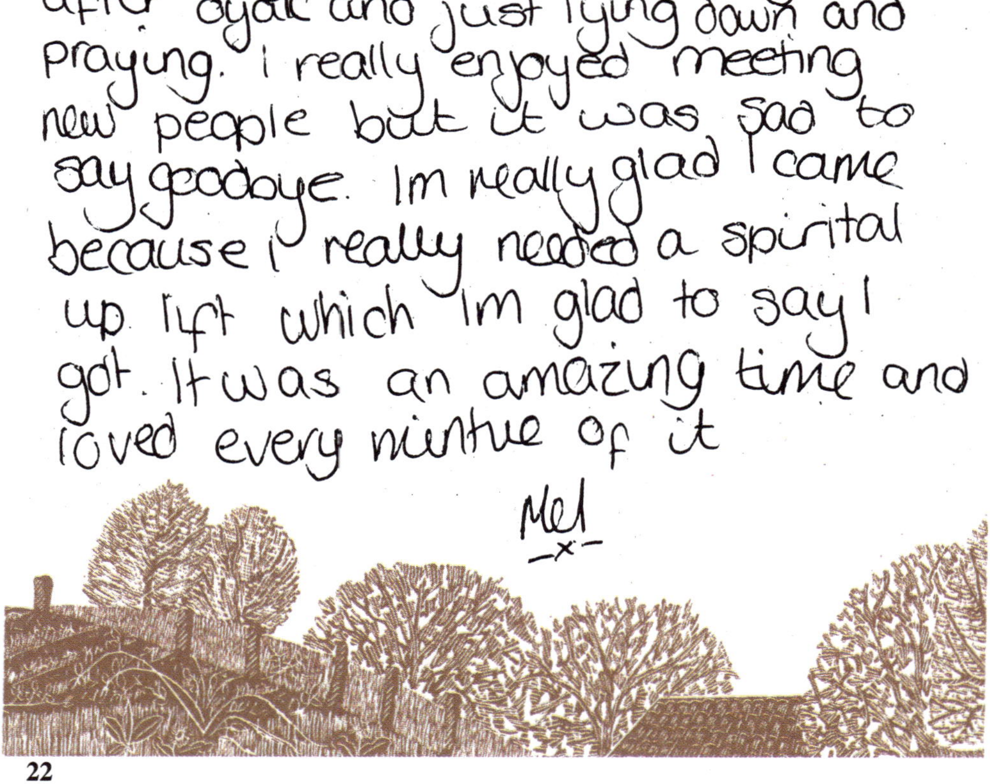

Wow! What an amazing week. So many
things have happened, I don't know where
the time went. To me, Taizé is just a
completly different world. No-one worries about
what you look like, what you sound like or
how you act. Its just so normal. The feeling
of the whole place here is just amazing.
It's so calming and peaceful. Everybody here
is so different to each other. Everyone gets
along even if you dont understand. The friends
I've made this week are amazing people, and
some of them have really touched my heart.
Even when I was down, just seeing some of them
made me so much happier. The past week
for me has been a bit of an emotional
rollercoaster. When making new friends have made
me happy, missing my closet mates back
home have made me sad.
I went through a time in the middle of
the week when I felt real bad. As I sat
in the church late at night, just
listening, watching and thinking
everything became clear

All the problems that I've had in the short 15 years of my life all made sense. It seemed to piece together like a jigsaw. For me this made me see that for what I have got in my life, I should make the most of it. That night I felt that God touched me big time. I broke down in tears and was lost. I didn't know what to do. I had all these thoughts running through my mind of things here and at home. In a way, It was amazing. Then that brought me to a question. Where am I going in life? To me now, there is no answer. There is no way to explain this week. It's just so unreal. Just sitting here now, makes me think of what has happened and of the memories I have. As I look back on the week, it makes me upset to think that I could of made more of it. One thing I will take home with me is that 'God, you are incredible'.

Love Susan

xxxo

Youth Synod members performing a sketch at the daily reflections.

RAAAAAA

WOOOOOOOW! How awesomely amazing has this week been?! On Monday I was all for going home - I hated it. I didn't like the food, didn't understand the whole quietness thing. and there was no English people! I didn't understand why everyone loves it - but now ...! I didn't manage to get to the cross but the candle service wow! My knees were soaked by the end. I'm sure God was trying to say something but I haven't worked out what yet. Perhaps it'll all become clear soon?!

I didn't realise that it's so simple to live a calm, relaxed way. Taizé is definitely the place to work that out. But really, what's with the the bowls used as cups? No, seriously, it's been so much fun, and I've learned so much. For instance:

Mein hut der hat drei ecken,
Drei ecken hat mein hut,
Und hat er nicht drei ecken,
Dann wär es nicht mein hut!

Ich bin verruckt!
(I'm crazy!)

mein hut

If not with you, then I'll go with my family!

Perhaps again sometime?

PS - up top

God bless Jess
—x—

Well wow 1 week gone already thats scary. This week has had the most amazing vorship ever. I really feel completly changed in my faith. Hope someday we can go back. I really enjoyed the silences during the prayer, I found them really relaxing. But most of all I enjoyed the fellowship that existed between us and our foreign friends. God bless love

John - Steven Fry - Dylan

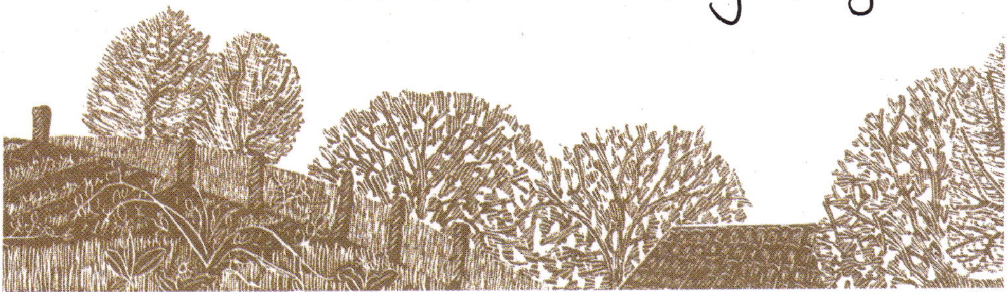

The Source (Monet's Garden!) - a scene of tranquillity at Taizé.

Well, um! Taizé really rox! I loved it last time I went, all I could say was "Amazing". This time, I feel I was lacking in faith a little, and the trip has just reminded me that God is ALWAYS there for us. Many things ~~struck~~ ~~Another thing which really~~ struck me this week; one was how there are so many young people all over the world who all beleive in the Saviour. Another thing which got me

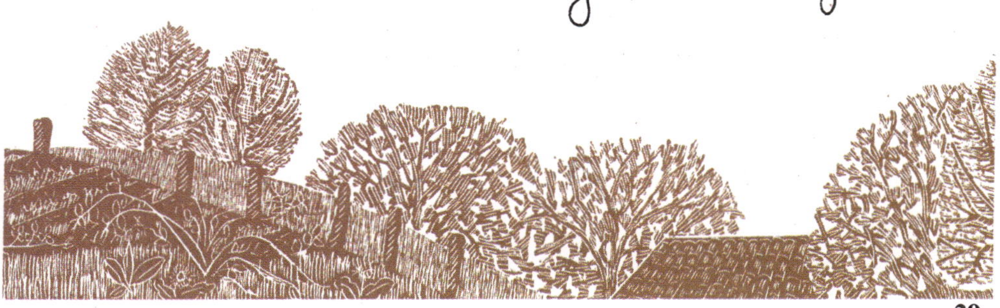

was how rubbish the English are at Languages! Oh, so we learnt the hat song ("Mein Hutt der hast drei ecken") but could anyone say as much in German as they did in English? I'm determined to break that barrier between Christians.

Um, Finally, I'm going back to Taizé, so anyone who wants to come back with me is welcome.
Ooh - I just thought: this week also unburdened me of all my troubles. I feel light at last.

Luv Amy xx

God bless

Can I just say that I love it when you put your foot in my face (ba da ba da ba da ba da)

How has Taizé affected me? well apart from being scarred for life from shit overflowing from toilets I would say that Taizé is a life changing experience. It has changed my outlook on a lot of things. I loved every second of it more than I can say (especially when I was with THOMAS) and it's one of my favorite places.

what's happened to me that I want to remember? Well experiencing a routine worship style was so awesome not sure at the mo how I'll cope. I want to remember everything at Taizé, it seems like a dream because it went by so fast. Apart from the peace most of I don't wana forget THOMAS, or 'Uncle Gary'. I loved all the singing as well from sing Songs with Andrew, screaming at Oyak, chanting and listening to Tracy Chapman with THOMAS! I think I've been really spoken to be God (in a good way) this week. Although unlike the hype of the holy spirit at soul survivor. I don't think I could name a specific time, but throughout the silences and worship and fellowship of THOMAS and everyone

else I really feel touched by God.
What have I discovered? Quite a lot actually. Mainly that I should really learn German! Nah.. the whole experience made me search myself and view worship and cultures in a completely new way. I could right a book about Taize cuz I loved it so much, but I'll stop now.
btw.. you're all invited to mine + THOMAS' wedding -

Good bless

Hannah Hedgehog

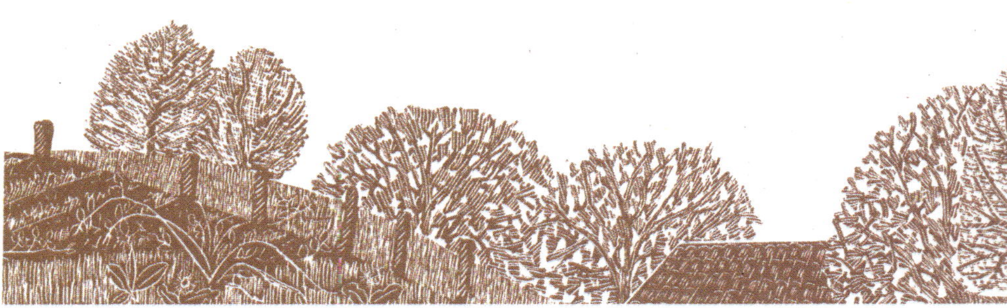

Oh Gary! Lol, so many happy memories from this week! Taize has shown me that being silent really helps for God to speak to me, so im going to try and do some quiet times each week. Something i always want to remember is the buzz of all the different cultures together talking, singing and laughing together. I feel that God has spoken to me in many ways but I can't pinpoint the moments.

♫ Dring Dring Dring, Cycle Gary ♫

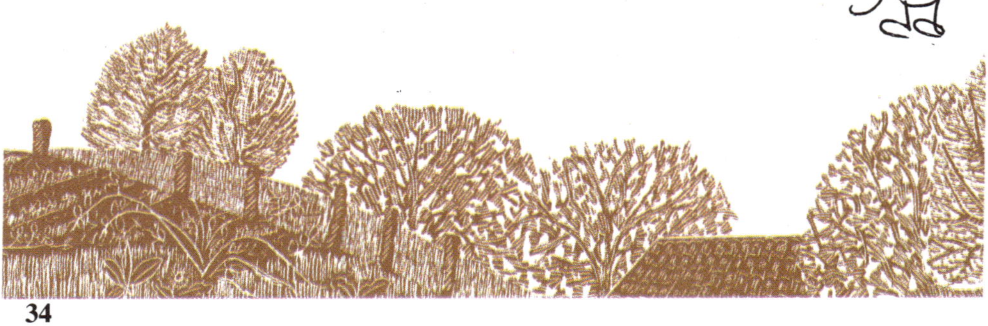

①

Taize is full of surprises, challenges, and is lots of fun! I never realised that being in a monostry, ontop of a hill in france would make me feel so comfertable, and safe, even though i have no idea how to get home! (but im sure it will involve many, many, forms of transport! I've learn't alot from the brothers, their simplistic way of life and their consistancy. Sometimes i wish i could never leave, but i know i do not have their level of control, especially over how i act...

I love tle wonderfil worship, It brings people together, and brings me to this deep level of thort and understand, all problems or conserns - like exams seem to melt away. I feel so calm and relaxed.

The people who you meet here are always lovely, all looking for simular things to yourself. So everyone understands, and you feel so able to share. Even people in dinner ques, you can just start a conversation and not have to worry.

(3)

The bible study and group
work is always enjoyable
in my group are lots of germans
and a french girl(s) and my leader
is from Jersey and only speeks
in English - hard to lead im sure - so
~~Germans~~ so everyone helps each
other to understand. Our sketch
in multiple languages "free oranges"
was loved by all! folge mir
After worship ojak opens, and
everyone meets for this odd
partylike thing, with fast food,
and 'men' playing guitar and huge
conga lines. I loved it all!
(ich liebe Johannes!)
Emma xx

J.S
4
9.V

Waterfall at The Source.

Wow... well I loved Taizé last time I came and I'm definitely coming back again. I don't know what it actually is about Taizé that affects peoples' faith so much but I know that, like last time, it has made me think about my faith and has strengthened it deeply.

Taizé is like a whole nother world and I can't believe we're going home already. its an absolutely amazing place because it helps everyone individually in different ways but you can make friends you'll keep forever.

I was a little worried when I last left Taizé that when I came back again it wouldn't be such a life-changing

PTO

and faith-changing experience a second time but I realised that I don't have to be in Taizé to find God because God is in me, with me & by me all the time anyway – Taizé is just where I can feel that way with 5,000 other people.

Thank you so much Andy & Helen, Steve Jacquie & Lorraine for organising it.

Love Lauren
-x-

Mon.

An opportunity for contemplation of a spiritual journey a time of focus + reflection, amongst a mass of energetic humanity. Several personal challenges at different levels. Not only have I survived but I have a wealth of positive experiences :- The beauty of the countryside, white blossoms, stone buildings, Brother Roger's Grave, covered in flowers. Frosty 6.30 a.m's, sunrises. Starry nights + moon. a blue tit nesting in a broken pole on the main path. The sense of deep peace within the church. + the wonderful moments of silence, + feeling the focused energy of 5,000 people. The ~~[illegible]~~ pearls of wisdom from the brothers. I approach my new changes with renewed + deepened faith in God.

Lorraine.

I Loved Taize!

Ich Liebe Taize!

J'adore Taize!

what else can I say?

from ~~[illegible]~~

Nate

The Girls from Germany are so nice!

The Girls from Ireland are also nice

The Girls from France rock

The Girls from England are cool!

Gott Preise, Liebe Nate

(means "GOD Bless Love Nate)

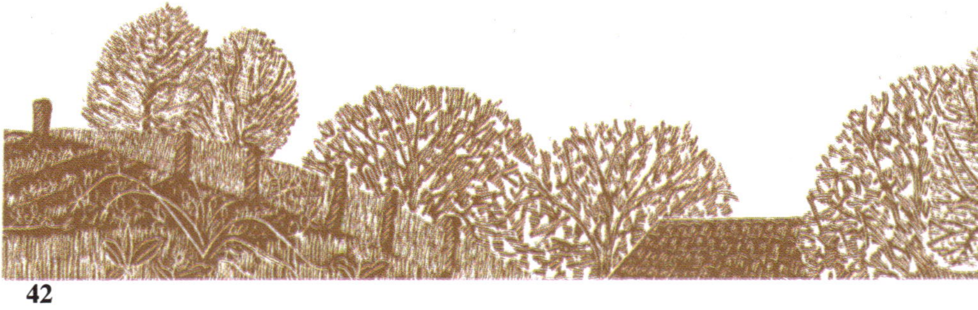

Reminders of Tezaie:

"Nice carpet"

FOOT GAME

◦Lucies monolog◦

"This is a story of my bunni"

"There's a speedboat on the lake! No its a car ....."

drinking from a bowl

"That suitcase sounds like a plane"

"Ohhh Hamish" "Ah my bra"

"Lush!"

"This is a spoon. A what. a spoon. this is a spoon"

Psyco Garry or cycle?

"Im going down"

Hummm:

Well Tezaie has definatly been an experience, I didn't understand the whole worship song stuff at the start but that cross service really shawed me the imporance of silence and its something I'll take home with me... along with some very groovy photos. You guys all rock & remember - imposibility is only a word.

Luv Beca the bear!

PS: Thankyou for making
my birthday so amazing
you are all so sweet
Im so happy to have met
you - singing at oyak was
the first time any one had
surprised me with singing
happy birthday - Youve
made history,

always
Becca

Entangled Group playing foot game!

Taizé has got to be one of my favourite places on earth. I've never had the urge to make a list before, but now I think about it Taizé must be in the top 3. I feel this Taizé Experience will be one that lasts in my memories a long time. However, I don't plan to put this to the test for too long 'cause I totally want to get back there!

It really communicated to me how great it is to be in a community of Christians; faith doesn't have to be introverted + one can be just as vocal about it as any other part of life (including songs about feet!). Sorry for bad handwriting, this is written on plane + I'm worried 'bout running out of time – we're almost home! Another thing 'bout Taizé is that I felt at home really quickly

So every day was enjoyable and I didn't feel any trouble fitting in; though I guess I should really thank you guys for that latter point.

I plan to tell everyone about Taizé when I get back, so hopefully they'll have lots more pilgrims in future!

love from
Sarah
(the new girl)

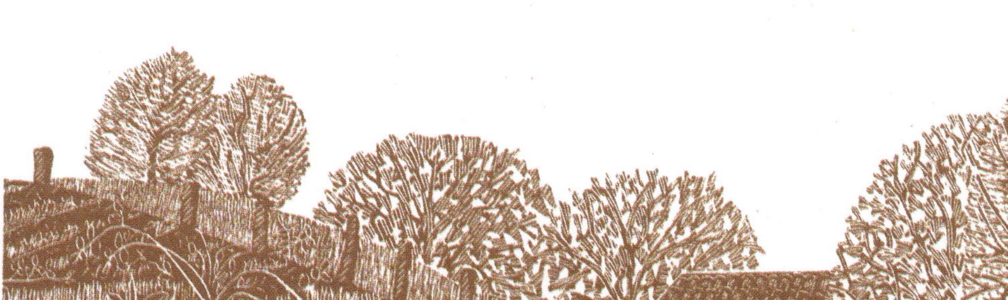

Hey Gaza! Well... to be honest I wasnt
really looking forward to Taizé because
I thought it would be a bit of a
drone. But now I have been I think
its amazing! I can't believe how fast
this week has gone by! I really don't [illegible]
to leave, it feels like home now. I
think the silences really helped me to
open shut doors which were kept locked
I had quite an emotional time during
the middle of the week but was cleared
up quite easily which I didnt think
could happen. The atmosphere in Taizé is
just so peaceful and relaxed. I had no
thought or worry about the coursework
and exams I have ahead of me. I
loved the fact that basically everyone
was foreign, I liked finding out about
different cultures and I made so many
new friends. I'll never forget all of the →

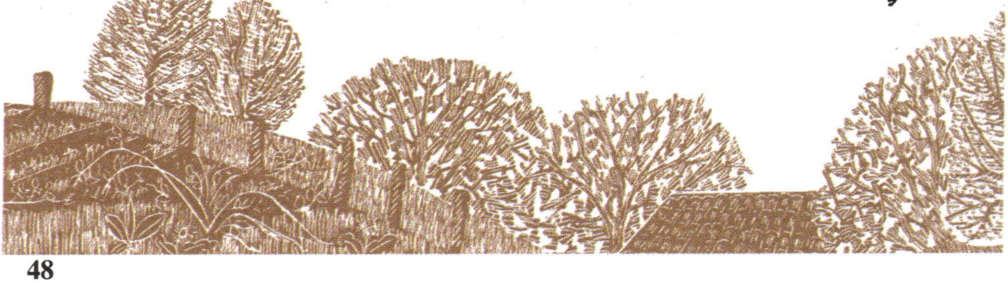

songs we were taught by the germans and the cycle garry song! lol! They are unforgettable! I think I found that to make a community, language barries are not an issue everyone just mixes with everyone which doesn't happen in many places. I really want to come back again! We need another trip Gaza!

Love

Laura xx

Small group at The Source.

The first time I went to Taizé I dreaded going – I hate crowds, I'm not good in the heat and I knew I was capable of being bored by Taizé chants! But the place, the worship, the brothers, the people and, of course God, all had their special effect on me; just like so many others before me it was on many levels, life changing.

This time, I knew it would be a different experience – and yet the same because Taizé has an amazing feeling of timeless, endless continuity of worship, work and play. It is such an amazing place of contrasts too. That among 5000 people I can find personal space, peace and time for reflection is awesome.

I particularly enjoyed, on this visit, camping as a group, the feeling of our group community as part of the larger community. →

So much of our worship in England is lacking in time of silence, I sometimes feel God must feel he is being nagged and want to say 'Shut-up you lot, just listen for a change!' Silence in the worship at Taizé can be so powerful, sometimes I felt it was just me and God and other times it felt like an amazing 'en masse' listening to God.

The simplicity of life at Taizé is wonderfully refreshing, a shedding of clutter and unnecessary matercail things – that so many can be fed simply but satisfyingly is miraculous. As always when away with young people there is so much to be learnt from them and to reflect upon. They were a great group.

Thank you Andrew & Helen
Jacquie

Andrew's diary – Postscript

This week has been amazing. So many great memories to take home. But it's more than just memories - things seem to happen in this remote corner in France that are of life affirming and life changing significance. Quite simply God is alive and at work here, and His presence becomes more and more visible through the lives of those who are present.

At the beginning of the week, I felt a sense of sadness that Brother Roger would be missing. How wrong I was! His spirit seemed more alive than ever through the sheer zest for life being lived out in front of me. It is a remarkable testament to the Community that after such an horrific event there can be such a sense of peace, acceptance and forgiveness about what happened. This truly is a life of reconciliation being lived out through the grace of God.

I have felt God touch me very deeply this week, and in many different ways. It has been incredibly rewarding and humbling to see how a group of young people from Cornwall can grow so deeply, in what initially seems such an alien environment. And to see that alien environment transform into a place of welcome, discovery, and a glimpse of heaven on earth.

For part of the week I was facilitating a group of fifteen and sixteen year olds from Germany, France and America. One of them, a girl called Nina, said very little at the beginning of the week. By our last meeting she seemed completely transformed. She spoke of how she was lacking in self confidence at the start of the week, but by the final day she shared this amazing sentence with the rest of the group - "I want to live only for God after this week in Taizé".

God has also caught me by surprise. I found Him speaking to me in a very powerful way through the Eucharist (Communion) service on Sunday morning. Prompted by the resurrection accounts of Jesus appearing to his friends on the Emmaus road, it struck me that Jesus reveals who he is through the giving of Himself to others. When He broke the bread their "eyes were opened" (Luke 24,v31). Even the resurrected Jesus walks with us, alongside us. He doesn't impose Himself, He waits to be invited in. I felt for the first time in my life that God was actually giving Himself to me through the sharing of bread and wine. The symbols of death – the body and blood of Christ-bringing new life through forgiveness on the cross, and everlasting hope through the power of the resurrection. Can there be a more significant or extraordinary transformation?

So as we go home I feel challenged as to how we can widen our visions and be a presence of God's hope in the world where we are. This isn't the end of an adventure, it's merely a beginning...... Maybe it could be for you too.

Andrew

Visiting Taizé form the UK:-

For precise details on how to get to Taizé (including rail timetables), or for any more information about the Taizé Community, be certain to check out the Taizé website: www.taize.fr

Part of the fun of taking a trip to Taizé is the journey (honest!). It's not altogether straight forward by public transport, but the actual process of travelling on several different types of transport is great for gelling a group Here follows a brief summary of the main travel options. Travelling in a large group (with lots of equipment) across Paris in the rush hour by metro is possible (we just about managed it), but isn't to be recommended! If possible try to cross Paris at non peak times.

Four main ways of getting there:-

Eurostar: The Eurostar runs from London to Paris through the Channel Tunnel. Trains are frequent and leave from Waterloo (shortly to change to St. Pancras) arriving at Paris Gare du Nord. Some services stop at Lille where it is possible to change onto the TGV network and board a train to Lyon Part Dieu. A local train runs from there back to either Mâcon Ville or Mâcon-Loché where there is a connecting bus to Taizé. If arriving at Paris Gare du Nord, you need to change onto an RER train (super metro) on either the route